Reflections

by Emily Madill

Always Believe in Yourself and Dream Big!

A Compilation of Inspirational Articles

For my Mom, thanks for helping me to believe that anything is possible and to always dream big. xo

"Mothers hold their children's hands for a short while, but their hearts forever." ~ Author Unknown

ISBN: 978-0-9881273-1-9

This book printed in the USA on paper that contains no fibre from old-growth forests.

Special thanks to Adrienne Madill Photography, Concept Photography and Kelli Etheridge Photography for capturing some of our great moments.

PLEASE NOTE: Every attempt has been made to properly attribute quotes included within the text of these articles. Any suggestions of how to more accurately attribute a particular quote can be directed to the publisher for future editions.

Note from the Author:

Hi, my name is Emily and I am an inspired Mother and Writer.

Having my two sons and entering motherhood has been the most amazing and transformational experience of my life. My boys have inspired me to follow my own dreams of writing. I want to be the best person and role model I can be for them. I hope to show them the importance of following their dreams and always believing in themselves. I balance my role as Mom with writing and creating.

My writing venture began over 5 years ago when I wrote and published a series of esteem building books for children. This project was inspired by my son Joe and resulted in starting a small book business called Em & Boys Books (EM & JOE BOOKS CO.). Since starting down this creative path, I had my second son Jake and have launched the 'Grateful Jake' story book and resource guide to help children and their families foster an 'Attitude of Gratitude'. Along my journey of writing for children I discovered blogging and my love for writing inspirational articles.

I really enjoy writing about my learning and 'aha moments' I experience along my journey of pursuing my dreams. My wish is that through sharing my writing, others will be inspired to believe in themselves. This booklet is a compilation of my favourite articles to date. I hope the readings will provide some comfort and encouragement, while portraying that we all share a common thread as each of us has a worthy gift to share with the world.

table of contents

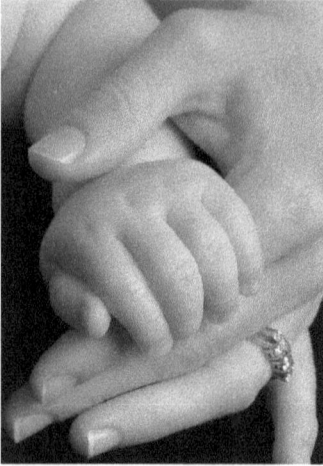

Getting Uncomfortable

Some of my most cherished experiences and achievements have been the result of entering into a world so uncomfortable and foreign my stomach would turn at the mere thought of having to go there. Have you ever entertained the idea that you'd rather be in the hospital rendered unconscious than get in front of an audience and speak out loud? Well I have, and this is the kind of discomfort I am talking about. Six years ago I was 26, recently divorced and in a new and healthy relationship with my now husband. By day I worked in an office for a busy construction rental company and by night I was glued to my computer determined to complete enough online courses to finish my degree. As though I wasn't sleep deprived enough I would rise at the crack of dawn and go for my morning run in an attempt to clear my head. Often during my morning runs I would visualize myself giving inspirational speeches and sharing words of wisdom to large audiences. This was always followed by great rounds of applause and awards of recognition for my accomplishments. I think this ritual was my way of making the run, which was usually cold and rainy, go by quicker.

Oddly enough, it still came as a huge surprise when my counselor at Thompson Rivers University called me up one day and said, "I don't know what it is about you Emily but I just keep thinking you would be the perfect Valedictorian for this year's graduation". Please know I wanted more than anything to take part in graduation festivies and I secretly yearned to take this role on, but the overwhelming thought that this lady was outrageous enough to think I would actually get in front of a crowd of 500 people with a microphone to say something intelligent and inspirational had me seriously considering not attending my graduation at all. I would love to tell you this was one of those times I took the bold leap into ultimate discomfort and gave the speech of my life, felt like a champion, received an award etc. however this is not the case. Instead, I politely declined despite her urging. Then I attended graduation with my head hung and avoided meeting face to face with my counselor because I felt like a failure. I should add that while I have regretted not giving the speech ever since, it has given me a great point of reference and provided me with a valuable life lesson.

On the upside, I married Mr. Wonderful and three years ago we had our first son. It was then I began my journey into the "uncomfortable zone". Maybe it was prompted by the discomforts of labour, sleepless nights, bags under my eyes, or some of the other realities motherhood can bring. Perhaps it was just that deep down I knew it was time to start pushing through some things. I was no longer okay with feeling like I couldn't give the speech or having self-limiting beliefs that I wasn't good enough or didn't truly deserve success and happiness. I wouldn't wish this for my son and if I were going to be his role model I knew I needed to muster up the courage to be the kind of role model he deserves. I enrolled in some amazing programs through Excellence Seminars International, a company that believes in the importance of stepping out of your comfort zone. I was sick about going because I heard I might have to talk in front of a crowd or something off the wall like that. I went anyway and after the first program I actually joined Toastmasters. Then an unbelievable thing happened, when I was in front of an audience speaking, I actually felt good and found some enjoyment in the whole experience. What I found even more surreal was that people actually wanted me to succeed and win and they were all incredibly supportive. As time marched forward, I took some major courageous steps in all areas of my life because each time I did I learned it wasn't nearly as bad as I had anticipated and the reward on the other side was always a feeling of immense confidence and pride. Much like a snowball effect, the more I stepped out and got uncomfortable the easier it became and the outcomes were incredible. The best part is I began believing in myself and became crystal clear on my purpose and the gifts I have to share with others.

During the first year and a half of my son's life, I wrote and self-published a series of inspirational children's books intended to empower young people to whole-heartedly believe in themselves. It wasn't a simple or easy undertaking. It involved many late nights knowing I would be up in a few hours to care for my baby. It required me to ignore the glazed over looks my well-meaning family and friends would give when I'd excitedly tell them of my venture. On more than a few occasions it demanded I slay my personal dragons, aka my self-limiting beliefs: "Who do you think you are?" and "This is never going to amount to anything, you should give up." Bit by bit I pushed through all that was uncomfortable in order to move forward and reach my goal. My book launch was a chance to share what I had created with others, but most of all for me it was an

overwhelming feeling of pride and disbelief that "I actually did it"; almost as though all along I was proving to myself that I could. The notion of becoming more comfortable with getting uncomfortable has shaped my world into a magical place. The journey of creating my small book business has led me down new paths of possibilities and dreams I never knew I had. It has provided me with the balance and self-fulfillment I wouldn't have if I had chosen to stay comfortable and complacent. On top of that, it has given me a forum to continue my practice of getting uncomfortable, strengthening my spirit and maintaining a healthy belief in self. I feel like I have the best gig going.
I also get to be the stay at home Mom of two sons now, Joe three years old and Jake who just turned one. My ultimate dream is that all of this will help empower my two young sons to believe they too can achieve any and all of their dreams no matter how uncomfortable the steps may first appear to be.

em

Gratitude:
the Power of Perception

I often wonder how it's possible for people to have abundance in many areas of their lives, and yet still seem so incredibly unhappy with their lot in life. On the flipside, I find it equally intriguing that there are just as many others in the world who have endured great suffering and loss; those that have very little in the way of physical comforts and things and nevertheless are happy, at peace and thankful each day for everything they do have. How does this work? What is the deciding element behind being content and happy with who we are and what we have?

Well, I wouldn't for a second claim to be an expert in this matter and preach how things are or are not; how people should or shouldn't be. I am just curious, so my theory as tested on myself time and time again goes like this. When I choose to, I can make a long list of things that I love about my life, myself and the people in my life...yes, each and every person in my life (past, present and future). I can also when I choose to, find the same amount of things that I wish were different about my life, myself and the people in my life. It is all dependent on my perspective and the particular lens I view myself and my life through.

12

Now I don't know about you, but for me the very idea that I possess the power within myself to choose how I feel about my life is empowering and a comfort in itself. On top of that, I have learned 'how I feel' serves as a strong indicator for what particular outlook I am operating under. Now I am not saying that there aren't situations and circumstances in life that warrant feeling sad, unhappy, mad or less than grateful for what lies before us. Life can get messy and there are always going to be things that don't make sense, that seem unfair, or feel unbearable.

I guess my point is when I want to feel good all I need to do is look around me for clues. They are everywhere in everything and in everyone. To me, being grateful doesn't mean sweeping all that is messy under the rug in an attempt to avoid or deny what is less than desirable and instead only see what is desirable. Rather, it is looking at the whole picture of life and instead of 'only focusing in' on what isn't good or isn't working, it is saying yes I see that and look there are also just as many things that are great, work pretty fine and that I wouldn't trade for anything. I can wholeheartedly say I would not trade places with anyone, anywhere. I am so thankful for my life, my people and my inquisitive mind that keeps my view on life interesting by offering continuous opportunities to stumble, learn and grow.

"Gratitude makes sense of our past, brings peace for today, and creates a vision for tomorrow."

Melody Beattie

em

Being Fabulous

*"Our deepest fear is not that we are inadequate.
Our deepest fear is that we are powerful beyond measure.
It is our light, not our darkness that most frightens us. We
ask ourselves, Who am I to be brilliant, gorgeous, talented,
fabulous? Actually, who are you not to be? You are a child
of God. Your playing small does not serve the world. There
is nothing enlightened about shrinking so that other people
won't feel insecure around you. We are all meant to shine, as
children do. We were born to make manifest the glory of God
that is within us. It's not just in some of us; it's in everyone.
And as we let our own light shine, we unconsciously give
other people permission to do the same. As we are liberated
from our own fear, our presence automatically
liberates others."*

Marianne Williamson

These wise words give me chills every time I read them because their truth resonates to my core. I remember the first time I read them I had a mix of emotions: 'Relief' that it really is acceptable and a great thing to be fabulous and to own and cherish my fabulousness... 'Grief' for time I wasted shrinking... 'Elation' that a simple shift in my belief system could have such a powerful effect in how I feel and how I show up in the world... 'Eager' to share the gift of these words and the meaning behind them with as many people as possible.

I really do believe that we are all born gifted and we are meant to share the gift of 'Who We Are' with others. I would never dream of telling one of my children they are anything short of magnificent; and I wouldn't dare tell them they should consider being less than who they are, or allow fear to stand in the way of accomplishing their dreams. Children pick up on cues from their peers and adult role models around them... so if I want to encourage my sons to take pride in 'who they are' as individuals and NOT allow fear to prevent them from believing in themselves- then I too must walk this path.

What makes ME fabulous is my honesty and willingness to share my journey and light with the world, in spite of the fear of putting myself out there...what makes YOU fabulous?

em

Being True to Me

Why is it that the people who are the least supportive and accepting are often the ones we most want to please and gain acceptance from? At least this has been the case in my life. Without getting too ahead of myself, I would like to give a bit of gratitude for my amazing life. I have a wide network of cheerleaders who love and accept me however I show up. I have some extraordinary mentors who help guide me and lift me up when I fall. I have 'the best' Mom a daughter could wish for. She is a no-drama, real deal kind of lady who can in a couple of sentences help me get unstuck from the stickiest of situations. My husband is by far my biggest fan and supporter and my two beautiful sons are my source of inspiration. These fine fellas in my life never fail to provide me with ample learning opportunities to grow as a person and as a woman. Like I said, I am 'very' fortunate. With all of this love and support I am surrounded with, some may ask, "How could she get stuck or worry about what others think?"

While I would admit this is a very good and valid point, I would also have to say there are obviously some repeat lessons I am still learning. For a good portion of my life, I have been a 'people pleaser'. I can distinctly remember at a young age setting out to do things as a means of receiving favorable reactions from others around me. Like a cause and effect experiment, I discovered early on that when I conducted myself in a certain way I was met with approval from others. I don't think this is an abnormal or unique trait, in fact I think as women and as humans we all want to be loved and accepted. What I have noticed is that some women show up exactly as they are; you either love them or you don't. They are okay either way. They are sincere and can be found living life with purpose, passion and acceptance of all those around them. These authentic types are honest and upfront and address their issues with the source directly. Sure like everyone they too have their struggles but, what I find most intriguing is these genuine ladies don't concern themselves with gaining acceptance from the Negative Nellies in their lives. They choose to spend their energy wisely and intentionally.

I have come to realize that there have been times all throughout my life I desperately sought the acceptance of the Nay Sayers. I guess I thought if I could get the people who are critical of everyone to say I was okay then it would really mean something. I would actually set out to 'people please' the people who aren't pleased with anything. Talk about going in circles! Eventually, after many dizzying repeat lessons I am learning about the importance of standing in my own power.

I now find myself in my early thirties in a significant role as a stay at home Mom of two healthy and 'very' active boys. I consider myself to be energetic with enough stamina to match the pace of my toddler and preschooler. I am fortunate to be able to give a lot of myself and energy to raise my family in the best way I know how. I also look forward to date nights and time spent sustaining a happy and healthy relationship with my husband. I value my time spent with close friends and family and doing things that are just for me. This brings me to my 'Aha Moment of Truth' and the start of a journey down a lighter path.

I finally began to see that when I would spend so much as one millisecond attempting to please the displeased, I would start depleting my precious energy resources I depend on to create a happy balance in my life. I also began to notice a pattern where my energy to 'people please' would come from. Naturally, I would first take it away from the things I do for myself. Then I would take it from my important relationships. Next if I wasn't really careful I would allocate it away from my marriage and my family. There I stood, defeated and deflated wondering what ever went wrong and why everything felt so hard all of the sudden.

I guess what I am getting at, is it no longer made any sense to spend an ounce of my energy caring, wondering or hoping for the approval of anyone but 'myself'. I realized if I want to live an authentic life with joy I must choose to stop giving my power away to the Nay Sayers. I still find it hard to wrap my brain around the idea that there will always be people out there that don't get me or perhaps don't like me, but I am learning that as long as I am true to myself it just isn't my concern. I definitely don't have it all figured out and at times I find it very challenging to not revert back to my 'people pleasing' tendencies. I get the feeling it is the human in me that will always to some extent want to please others as a means of gaining their approval. As my sons' role model I am striving to send the message to them that it's most important to gain the approval of yourself first and to try to stand in your power as much as possible when faced with negativity.

Moving forward, I sincerely wish for me and everyone else out there trying to break free from 'people pleasing' that more time is spent owning, expressing and loving ourselves the way we are. This alone could create opportunities for our authenticity to shine through for everyone to witness and enjoy. Who knows maybe in the process this action will also inspire the most powerful Nay Sayers to do the same.

em

Joy is a Gift
Available to Us All

Even though it may sound a little strange or quirky, I really do believe I write my own stories in life. Sure there is some kind of power beyond my realm of understanding I'm operating under and countless things in life I have absolutely no control over - I am okay with all of that. I am just saying, I wake up each morning as the author and creator of 'my life' and I like it. I may have little say in the overall happenings of the world, but I do have 'all' the say in how I choose to react to the things presented to me on a daily basis.

Under this belief system, I get to decide on the level of joy in my life. Sounds pretty basic and easy to attain and that's because it is. Yet however irrational it may seem, there are still times when the story I create for myself is the very thing preventing me from experiencing the limitless joy I have available

> *"Joy is what happens to us when we allow ourselves to recognize how good things really are."*
>
> Marianne Williamson

20

to me. What was once a straightforward feeling suddenly becomes a way of being that doesn't even register on the radar. The cloud of doom and gloom can be powerful and all encompassing. The stories and reasons I create for being caught under the cloud always seems so justified. Unfortunately the only person suffering from the convincing dismal story is the person creating it. So how do I get out of it once I am stuck in it? Well this is the best part, as the artist of my life, I know better than anyone what makes me feel happy and brings me joy. The world is beautiful and complex; there are many ways to help me recognize how good life really is. The criteria is different for everyone, how I create my joy is unique to me.

> *"The more light you allow within you, the brighter the world you live in will be."*
>
> Shakti Gawain

What I mean is we are all on a solo journey. No matter how interconnected and bonded we are with others, nobody really knows our every waking thoughts and feelings as well as we know ourselves. We can try to explain our story as we see it to others, but it seems silly to expect another person with completely different experiences, thoughts and feelings to grasp 'exactly' what we are saying and meaning. There is often a general understanding that we share with others but everyone is on their own path and journey. So what brings one person joy is unique to their story and journey. The joy must be created by the storyteller and not something we rely on others to provide us with.

This brings me back to my original statement that I write my own stories in life. I react to my own experiences in life. These reactions will either feel good or they will not feel good. If they feel good, great! If they don't then I must find my joy - it's there for everyone to experience as much and as often as we want to experience it. To me, feeling happy and at peace is the best gift life has to offer. I find my peace and joy by taking the time to enjoy my boys, be with friends and family and reflect on all I am grateful for.

em

Pursuing My Dreams

"Don' t ask what the world needs. Ask what makes you come alive and go do it. Because what the world needs is people who have come alive"

Howard Thurman.

I love when I come across people who are excited and charged up about what they are doing in life. When people spend time immersed in what they are truly passionate about, they exude a level of enthusiasm that is contagious. The smile they wear as they speak of their passion is bright and powerful. I find myself so intrigued I can't help but hang on every word as they describe what it is they love to do. A short conversation with an empowered individual inspires me to continue following my dreams of writing. I feel very fortunate to have discovered that writing is a powerful outlet that brings me a sense of joy, accomplishment and connection with others. I love to dream big, and I have big dreams for my future and my writing. Knowledge is power so being aware and connected to what makes me come alive is a true gift in itself.

The next part of 'going out there and doing it' sounds simple enough. However, this is often the most common roadblock that prevents dreams from becoming a reality. Sometimes it's the uncertainty about where to start or an overwhelming sense of fear that can extinguish a dream before it has ever had the chance to take flight. I believe it is common to take on so many different roles and responsibilities in life that another familiar stopping place is being 'overcommitted'. "How can I possibly follow my dream when I hardly have time for what is already in front of me?" I believe the more compelling question to ask is: "How can I possibly choose to turn my back on my dream when I am so aware of what it is?" Holding myself back from what I know is important to me doesn't serve me or anyone else close to me.

I have learned two very important things while pursuing my dreams. The first one is the value in having support. I am fortunate to have some extremely solid relationships with people who truly know me and want me to win in my life. These are the people I turn to when I question my sanity for pursuing my dream and thankfully they are the ones who quickly remind me of the progress I have already made and the importance of continuing on. Having relationships with people who want to lift me up in life and who I would also support in a heartbeat is priceless. The other very important lesson I am learning is the effectiveness of taking 'baby steps'. When I look at the grand picture of how I am going to make my big dream a reality, I very quickly become overwhelmed. On the flipside, when I take one little step towards my dream, I begin to build my confidence and gain the courage to take the next step and move forward. I believe this is how dreams are actualized, with perseverance, dedication and remembering it doesn't need to happen all at once. I have learned it is essential to continue to believe in myself and my dreams; to trust the process that all is unfolding as it should and to never give up before a dream has come to life.

My husband's Grandpa Freddy lived to be 93. He was one of the most interesting characters and a true example of someone who lived his dream despite all odds against him. He used to recite these words to my husband from the poem "Never Quit" by an anonymous author. My husband was insightful enough to pass them along to me when I needed them most:

> Life is queer with its twists and turns,
> As every one of us sometimes learns,
> You never can tell how close you are,
> It may be near when it seems so far;
> So stick to the fight when you are hardest hit;
> It's when things seem worst that you must not quit.

For everyone out there pursuing their dreams, I hope these words provide a bit of comfort and encouragement to keep on your journey of passion and purpose.
The world will be a better place because you do.

em

Letting Go

> *"Some think it's holding on that makes one strong - sometimes it's letting go."*

Sylvia Robinson

There is something so freeing about letting go. Even the expression 'let go' reminds me of a well deserved sigh of relief. On a number of occasions I have found myself holding on to a thought, belief or situation with absolutely everything I am even when it doesn't feel good. It is only when I release my grip that feelings of peace and clarity flood in. If I am aware of the power in letting go of the things that don't serve me, why can it still feel like such a challenging mindset to apply? Naturally it all depends on what's at stake, as some things are much easier to forget and not feed energy into. Usually the things I am more emotionally invested in are more difficult to let go of.

I have been known to wear my heart on my sleeve and almost always root for the underdog. Wanting other people to feel good about themselves when they are struggling to see their greatness has always been something that makes me feel

26

good. Unfortunately, sometimes by my own doing I get a bit too caught up in other people's stories and misfortune and my desire to boost them back up often comes at the cost of my energy. When I am busy minding other people's business there is nobody here minding mine; this can very quickly become a problem. I am not doing myself or anyone else any favors by putting my life on hold in an attempt to improve their journey. In fact, by attempting to help others by cushioning their fall, I can get in the way of their learning, which is the exact opposite outcome I intended.

After coming to this realization, I figured there had to be a way to have the best of both worlds for me - to inspire others to feel good while also feeling great myself. That's when I realized by maintaining my focus and energy on 'my' passion and purpose, I am sharing my gift with others, while taking care of myself. This kind of "aha moment" is the perfect motivation for me to "set free" the relationships, situations and thoughts that bog me down and deplete my energy. Being true to myself to the best of my abilities is my offering and if others choose not to accept my offerings I must not take it personally by holding onto it.

The quote by Marianne Williamson that states: *"As we let our own light shine, we unconsciously give other people permission to do the same,"* really speaks to me. I believe that when we focus our energy and attention on ourselves and become aligned with who we are and what we have to offer, our world automatically becomes a richer and better place. This quote also reminds me that holding others 'as able' to figure out their own journey will have a much greater impact than believing I have any control over what path they will ultimately choose to take. All I really have control of is the person I choose to be on a daily basis. I am learning that the act of letting go can be a true test of courage and faith. Letting go of the belief I need to always do something to help those who appear to be struggling is liberating! I definitely recommend releasing the things that don't feel good to you. You too may be surprised by how uplifting it feels.

em

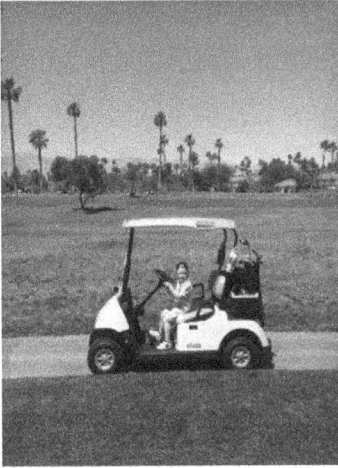

View from the Driver's Seat

*"It is much more valuable to look for the strength in others.
You can gain nothing by criticizing their imperfections."*

Daisaku Ikeda

I believe it is a normal part of human nature to develop opinions of the people, places and things we are surrounded by. We are constantly being bombarded with information. We take it in and then reshape it to fit with our own belief systems. This becomes a natural process that helps us make sense of what lies before us. Unfortunately the information we are presented with isn't always based on truth, it may be somebody's truth or opinion but not necessarily one that encompasses the whole story.

I have certainly been guilty of viewing others through a murky lens by forming opinions of them based on their unfavorable traits. I have also had the experience of changing my viewpoint of others by focusing my attention on their strengths and qualities I admire. When I choose to believe something, whether true or not, I'll search high and low to find evidence to back up my belief. I have yet to come across someone who lacks some kind of redeeming qualities that are admirable. I believe we all have strengths and an innate desire to be accepted and loved.

When I choose to view others through the lens that they also want to be loved and accepted, and I shift my focus to what I value about them, I very quickly find evidence that supports a more positive outlook. When I focus on what I enjoy about another person, I can't help but feel good. On the flipside, when I am being critical of others, I feel unsettled. I love the quote by Wayne Dyer that states: "When you judge another, you do not define them. You define yourself".

How I'm feeling about others can be a great indicator for 'my own sense of self-worth'. When I stay in tune with creating happiness for myself, I tend to have happy thoughts and opinions of others. When the opposite is true, I need only to look inside myself to make a shift in how I choose to see what lies before me. A great friend recently shared the 'car metaphor for life' with me, it goes like this: When things feel unsettled and you're not sure what's true, take a good look around yourself and see whose car you're in....if you find you're in the passenger seat or worse the backseat of someone else's car, get the hell out as quick as you can and get back into the driver's seat of your own car to gain control of the only thing you have control of ~ your life, your business and your happiness. Only then will you see things with a greater sense of clarity.

The view from my driver's seat is looking pretty darn good! Happy Driving Everyone.

em

Taking Action

> *"The grass is always greener where you water it."*

Author Unknown

I am a devoted 'To Do' list maker. When I 'focus' on creating a certain result in my life, whether personal or professional, I am more apt to take the steps that eventually help me reach my goal. The key for me has always been to write my goals down. Then each day I write down at least one thing I can do, no matter how big or small, that will help me get there. There are those who snicker and make fun of my quirky lists and 'Type A ' behaviour; however I find something very powerful in the act of putting pen to paper. Having my goals before me in such a visible and accessible format is a strong reminder to take action and keep my dreams in motion. When I put a dream, a goal or even a task on the back burner that is exactly where it stays. Life gets busy and there are always a number of things that pull me in different directions. When I take a good look around at the current state of my life and results I've created it becomes very obvious what kind of effort I've been

putting in. If I don't like what I see, I can 'course correct', take
action and move forward. If I'm happy with my results I trek
on. I like to believe we all can achieve our deepest desires and
dreams; it's a matter of believing we can, and then going out
and doing something about it. I don't feel success is limited to a
select few. Achieving personal accomplishments and attaining
dreams generally happens for those who take action and do
something to help make it happen. We all have our roadblocks
and obstacles to overcome on the journey of actualizing dreams;
some are faced with more obvious and challenging barriers
than others. The one constant is that the future isn't written
in stone. I believe I am an active participant in shaping my
future and I have a choice in how much effort and action I
apply in my life. I find Pema Chodron's quote: *"The future is
completely open, and we are writing it moment to moment"* to
be very inspiring. I am not suggesting that in order to take
action and achieve success everyone must write down their
goals, and carry around lists and reminders of what they will
do. There are many different techniques that support taking
action; do what works best for you. Whatever method we each
choose to take, may we all make the most of our moments
on the journey to reaching our deepest desires and dreams.

em

Being Mindful of My Words

"Because even the smallest of words can be
the ones to hurt you, or save you."

Natsuki Takaya

"If you can't say something nice, don't say nothing at all", famous words by Walt Disney's Thumper in the movie Bambi. This wisdom passed down from our furry friend is something most of us have heard as children or at some point in our lives. Each of us has likely been on the receiving end of hurtful words as well as taking on the role of dishing it out. I have never experienced a good outcome from uttering unkind words to another or about another. True, the instant gratification is usually very satisfying in a 'fiery' kind of way. Most often my unkind words are the result of feeling hurt or misunderstood, and that instant hit I get from vocalizing my pain is an attempt to feel better about myself. Unfortunately if my words are laced with pessimism or cruelty the end result is feeling unsettled, instead of at peace. This cycle, if not broken, can be so destructive on relationships with others, as well as on the one we all have with 'ourselves'.

33

I have found that too often people (myself included) can get caught up in the whirlwind of negative talk, not only about others but also about themselves. The power in words, whether communicated verbally or in written format is incredible. When I am around those who spend time complaining and gossiping about others, I leave feeling drained and defeated. When I am around people who have a happy demeanor or talk of life situations from a more optimistic and hopeful point of view, I leave feeling energized and clear.

I am not suggesting that every word I communicate from here on must be about rainbows and unicorns because lets face it, sometimes it is necessary to be bold and stand up for oneself. What I have observed and am still learning, is that delivering any kind of message can be done without being unkind or mean. Choosing carefully not only the words I speak, but also being clear on the intention behind them, may at first sound a bit unnatural or daunting; however I have found the effect of doing so to be empowering and very worthwhile.

I challenge everyone to try for one day or even for one hour, to be Mindful of the words you speak. To swallow unkind words whether they are about you, someone else, or a situation; instead, follow Thumper's law and either say 'nothing', or replace it with words that are of a kinder nature. The powerful effect it will have on your own state of being and the others around you will be contagious. I find when I follow Thumper's lead, negative barriers are removed and I realize I have a lot more in common with others than I may have previously thought. It is well worth the initial discomfort and periods of silence. Come on and give it a try!

"The real art of conversation is not only to say the right thing at the right place but to leave unsaid the wrong thing at the tempting moment."

Dorothy Nevill

© Etheridge Photographic

Hold the Vision;
Trust the Process

"Hold the vision, Trust the process." I find these words to be
comforting and inspiring, especially at the start of the year as
I prepare my vision and goals for the New Year. The practice
of visualization and goal setting is empowering. Carving out
this special time is a key ingredient to achieving my hopes and
dreams. Taking time on New Year's Day to create yearly vision
boards has become a family ritual that I always look forward
to. I enjoy designing a road map that helps me identify the
key areas of life I wish to succeed in. I try to stay away from
making a 'list of resolutions', as I find it doesn't hold the same
kind of emotional impact as creating a meaningful picture of
what is really important to me. Envisioning how I imagine
I'll "feel" when I achieve my goals is the main way I connect
to each area I wish to have more success in. This may sound a
bit hokey, but I really do believe setting intentions with some
emotional force helps to kick a dream into motion. I also give
gratitude for the many amazing things and people already in
my life. Feeling happy for where I currently am, is a mindset I
love because it sets me up to believe I am already winning in

my life. This way, what I am striving towards isn't something I need to delay my inner happiness or sense of achievement for; instead, it is about creating more of what I already have!

After being clear on my yearly vision, I design a poster board to showcase my meaningful statements, and goals. I display it in a special place, so it serves as a valuable reminder throughout the year to trust the process and continue making steps towards my goals. Trusting the process is every bit as important as defining what it is I hope to achieve. When I try to control my path too much, I close myself off to opportunities I had no idea existed. I've learned the more I am open and trust that I am on the best path for my continued happiness, the more magic happens in my life. If you haven't already, I recommend the art of creating vision boards for your upcoming year; this can be done at any time of the year. Remember to display your masterpiece proudly and trust that the magic of your own life will unfold as it should. I wish everyone happiness, health and success. Have fun & Dream BIG!

em

Family Gratitude Activity

"Gratitude unlocks the fullness of life. It turns what we have into enough, and more. It turns denial into acceptance, chaos to order, confusion to clarity. It can turn a meal into a feast, a house into a home, a stranger into a friend. Gratitude makes sense of our past, brings peace for today, and creates a vision for tomorrow."

Melody Beattie

I love this quote for its truth. When I look at any situation in my life through the eyes of thankfulness and gratitude I feel good...and isn't that what really matters in life - 'how we feel inside'. That said, adopting an "Attitude of Gratitude" at a young age is an asset and a life skill children will be able to use for a lifetime of happiness. I believe that in order to help my boys build an "Attitude of Gratitude" I will need to do more than teach them to say please and thank you. I keep a Gratitude Journal and it is an amazing tool to help look at the big picture of my life and feel happy and proud.

So if this works for me, I figure an adapted kid friendly journal is a great start for them! Both of my boys love arts and crafts, so I wanted to add this element. My eldest son is just turning five so a written journal is a bit out of his reach. He does have a fabulous imagination and a great way with words, so this is something we do together. We talk about what we are thankful for and what makes us 'feel' happy in our lives. Then he creates a picture about something he is thankful/grateful for and tells me about it and I add the description at the bottom. It is a great activity that builds his confidence up and creates an opportunity for us to connect and have fun together.

Create your Gratitude Journal any way you like. We had fun creating the Cover of my son's journal with pictures of some of the special people in his life he is grateful for. This helped him create a sense of ownership and pride in this activity from the get-go. Here are some Ideas:

· Use a store bought Notebook and add different pictures, magazine clippings, etc. to decorate the front. OR you could make a scrapbook style with Construction paper, it is yours by design. Be Creative and Have Fun!

· Make a Family Gratitude book where all members of the family can take turns adding notes, pictures, etc. of the things they are grateful for. This could be done on a yearly or continuous basis.

Emily's Recipe for Chocolate Macadamia Nut Cookies

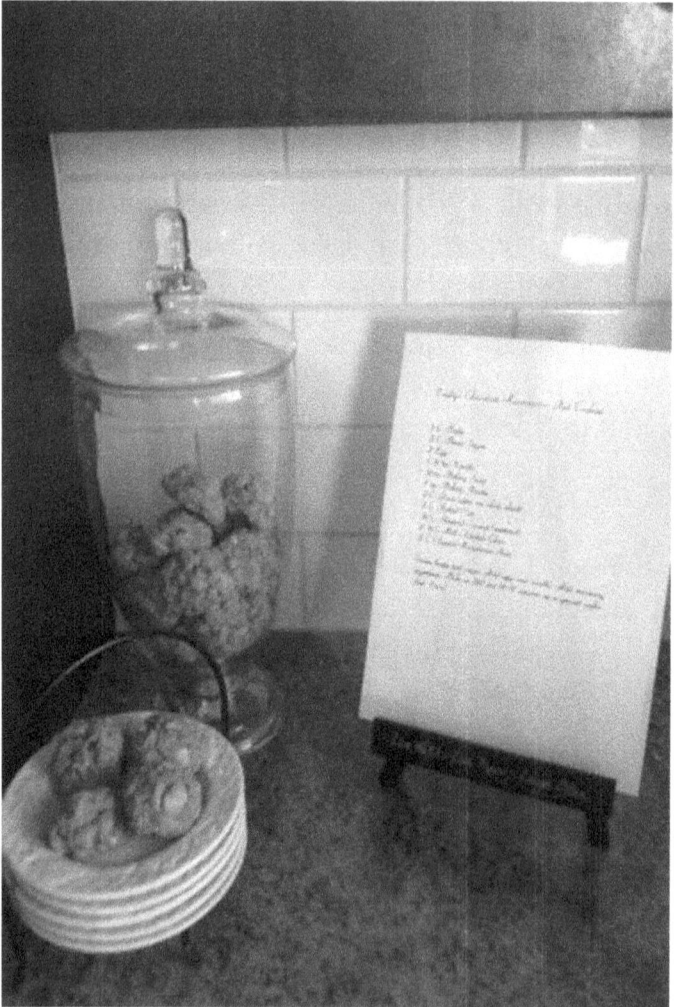

These cookies are a staple in our Cookie Jar
and a favorite for play dates and gatherings.

INGREDIENTS:

1 Cup Butter

2 Cup Brown Sugar

2 Eggs

1 1/2 tsp Vanilla

1 tsp Baking Powder

1/2 tsp Baking Soda

2 Cups Rolled Oats

2 Cups Flour (often use whole wheat)

2 1/2 Cups Milk Chocolate Chips

3/4 Cup Shredded Coconut (sweetened)

1 1/2 - 2 Cups Macadamia nuts

Preheat oven 350 Farenheit. Cream butter and sugar together, add eggs and vanilla, add rest of ingredients.

Form into balls and place on greased cookie sheet. Cook for 10 - 12 minutes and Enjoy!

Emily Madill

About the Author:

Emily lives on Vancouver Island, BC with her husband and two sons. She has a BA in Business and Psychology. Emily believes in the importance of teaching children accountability and empowerment from a young age. She enjoys writing and creating anything that will inspire others to believe in themselves. Being a mother is the most creative job she has had to date.

Emily is available for hire as a freelance writer and specializes in inspirational articles. She also focuses on fun ideas and activities to boost children's confidence in her 'Confident Kids are Cool' blog. For more information on Emily's work, please visit her website at:

www.emilymadill.com

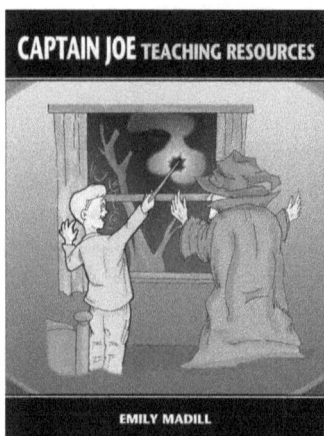

CAPTAIN JOE TEACHING RESOURCES

EMILY MADILL

About Emily's Captain Joe Series

The Captain Joe Series was designed as a tool for adults to teach children about constructive imagination. The four books are a fun and interactive way to introduce the concept of "Thoughts Turn Into Things" (so choose the ones that make you happy) to young children, ages five to nine years.

Joe and his thought-zapping superpower will invite children to use their imaginations to constructively choose thoughts that promote healthy self-esteem and self-awareness. Each story is designed to teach a key concept.

- *Captain Joe to the Rescue* is a great way to begin discussions with children around thoughts, attitudes and personal power in shaping them.

- *Captain Joe Saves the Day* is a great way to open discussions around the importance of following our dreams in an appealing way kids will relate to.

- *Captain Joe's Gift* is a great way to introduce discussions with children around standing up against bullying and celebrating our differences.

- *Captain Joe's Choice* is a great introduction to discussions around the power of our thoughts and choices in creating our happiness.

- *Captain Joe Teaching Resources* contains 100+ pages of lesson plans, worksheets and ideas to help parents and teachers extend learning based on all 4 Captain Joe books in the series.

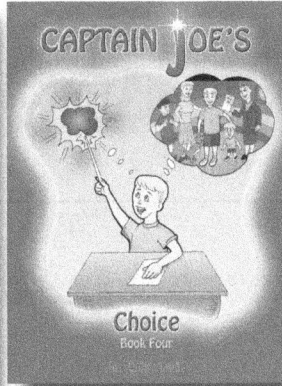

Available from Amazon and other online book sellers around the world.

iPad editions

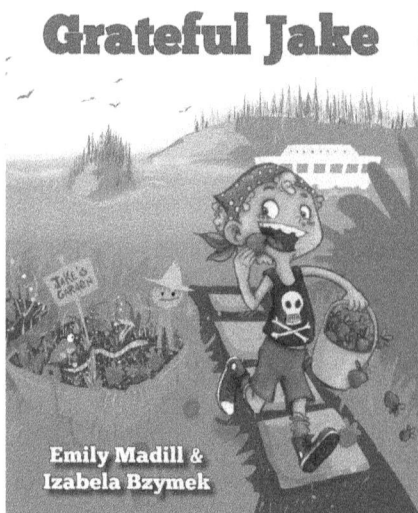

Available on the iBookstore

Print editions

Grateful Jake and the ***Grateful Jake Resource Guide*** available in print format from Amazon and other online retailers around the world.

Grateful Jake Resource Guide
is perfect for solidifying
children's awareness and
practice of gratitude and
encouraging them to begin
developing an 'Attitude
of Gratitude'. Suitable for
classroom use, home schooling
or to have some fun activities
to do together as a family!

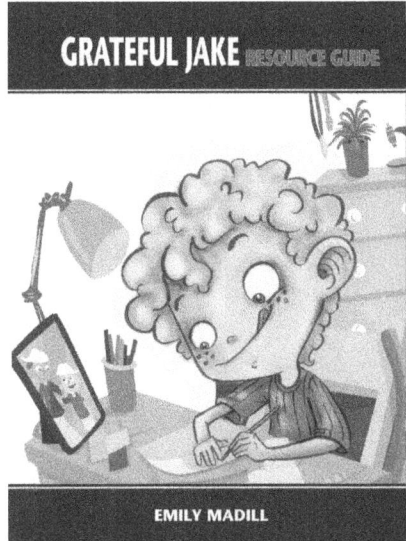

GRATEFUL JAKE RESOURCE GUIDE

EMILY MADILL

The guide includes:

* 12 different lesson
plans based on the Grateful Jake Book including a
variety of handouts to complement the lessons

* Additional resources, including a Math
Worksheet, Word Search, Vocabulary
list, and Story Sequence handout

* Comprehension, Word Study and
Critical Thinking worksheets

* Colouring Sheets

*Visit **www.emilymadill.com** for more activity ideas,
and complete info about Emily's books.*